Winner of the 2022 Cave Canem Prize
Selected by Willie Perdomo

Inaugurated in 1999 with Natasha Trethewey's *Domestic Work*, selected by Rita Dove, the Cave Canem Prize is an annual first-book award dedicated to the discovery of exceptional manuscripts of poetry by Black poets. Cave Canem is a nonprofit organization committed to cultivating the artistic and professional growth of Black poets. Founded by artists for artists, Cave Canem fosters community across the diaspora to enrich the field by facilitating a nurturing space to learn, experiment, create, and present. Cave Canem develops thoughtful audiences for Black voices that have worked and are working in the craft of poetry.

Black Pastoral

Black Pastoral POEMS

Ariana Benson

The University of Georgia Press
ATHENS

Published by the University of Georgia Press
Athens, Georgia 30602
www.ugapress.org
© 2023 by Ariana Benson
All rights reserved
Designed by Kaelin Chappell Broaddus
Set in 10/13.6 Quadraat OT Regular
Most University of Georgia Press titles are
available from popular e-book vendors.
Printed digitally

Library of Congress Cataloging-in-Publication Data

Names: Benson, Ariana, author. | Strange, Sharan, writer of foreword.
Title: Black pastoral : poems / Ariana Benson.
Other titles: Black pastoral (Compilation)
Description: Athens : The University of Georgia Press, [2023] | Winner of the 2022 Cave Canem Prize;
    Selected by Willie Perdomo.
Identifiers: LCCN 2023016548 (print) | LCCN 2023016549
(ebook) | ISBN 9780820365183 (paperback) | ISBN 9780820365190 (epub) | ISBN 9780820365206 (pdf)
Subjects: LCSH: Black people—Poetry. | Nature—Poetry. | LCGFT: Poetry.
Classification: LCC PS3602.E68525 B58 2023 (print) | LCC PS3602.E68525 (ebook) | DDC 811/.6—dc23/
    eng/20230503
LC record available at https://lccn.loc.gov/2023016548
LC ebook record available at https://lccn.loc.gov/2023016549

for the Black South—our fruit strange & sweet

So far from sweet real things my thoughts had strayed,
I had forgot wide fields; and clear brown streams
    —ALICE MOORE DUNBAR-NELSON, "Sonnet"

      why
is there under that poem always
an other poem?
     —LUCILLE CLIFTON, "surely i am able to write poems"

CONTENTS

II. **Black Pas**toral

III. **Black Pastoral**

Out beyond ideas of wrongdoing and rightdoing, there is a field. I'll meet you there.
When the soul lies down in that grass, the world is too full to talk about. . . .
—Rumi

FOREWORD

the earth is a living thing
. . .
is a black and living thing
is a favorite child
of the universe
feel her rolling her hand
in its kinky hair
feel her brushing it clean
                                   —Lucille Clifton

As a collection of poems concerned with liberation—the quest of our enslaved ancestors and of their 21st-century descendants, still—*Black Pastoral* contains the arc of an epic. As such, it also deals with temporalities in the sense of Tina Campt's "grammar of black futurity [that imagines] liberation *in the future anterior sense of the NOW* . . . the future [we] want to see right now, in the present." The term *black pastoral* posits an intimate relationship between blackness and the ideal of the pastoral—a natural landscape that is serene, idyllic, romantic, even beatific—and in doing so it evokes questions: How has Black presence contributed or been conscripted to creating such a space? In what ways has the notion of the pastoral included and delimited, defined and contorted Black presence? Conversely, does Black presence challenge and complicate a notion of the pastoral? What are present-future possibilities for a black pastoral? As Camille Dungy's anthology *Black Nature* (2009) makes clear, African American poets throughout history have variously affirmed our claims upon the natural world and its claims upon us. What does Ariana Benson's ecopoetics afford us, not only in investigating the *nature* of our relationship to nature (sometimes ambivalent) but also in embracing a state of awe and reverence—emblematic of that relationship and much more in the realm of black experience?

 In the geographical context of the U.S. South in which many of these poems are set—though certainly not limited to it—that intimacy is historically fraught with bondage, brutality, and blood, yet, as these poems show, with love, too . . . but not Romance, given the economies of violation and violent exploitation that have forged the relationship. The book's prologue introduces a through-line—a series of persona poems, all titled "Love Poem in the Black Field," that coalesces themes of history, identity, and nature, spiritually framing their relation to the Black body, to the existential stakes of blackness in the United States . . . (and, possibly, a post-terrestrial world?) They establish this collection's mythic and epic scale. With each reiteration of this poetic construct, Benson seems to suggest that, beyond its fundamental implication in Black survival, and as more than a requisite prism of our collective self-perception, Love might be more properly considered the ground of Black ontology. As Lewis R. Gordon has argued that blacks have been rendered "psychically homeless" in the West by its logic of white supremacist hegemonic oppression, consider then that black presence—our "Black Field" of persistence, our insistent *Being*—could be attributed to, even conflated with, a governing logic of Love. Thus, on its highest terms the *black pastoral* is conceptual representation and instantiation of that enduring logic (i.e., *Love* and *Black Field* as mutually constitutive energies). This is the kind of rumination, for me at least, that Benson's poems inspire.

The "Love Poem[s] . . ." set in the 19th century are especially poignant. They illuminate love under duress that enlivened as well as sustained those who gave and received it, during their lives and beyond. In the first of the series, a runaway addresses the beloved whom they had been awaiting:

> When you arrive to pull me up
> 　　　　From the mud, the salt will crumble
> From my eyes; my eyes
> 　　　　That, for nights, have seen
> Nothing, save that cardinal
> 　　　　North from which the stars beckon;
> Those stars that, like you, never fade
> 　　　　From sight, even in the day
> -Blue sky. Then, for weeks,
> 　　　　Unspeaking, we'll follow their call,
>
> 　. . .

. . . . Such silence
                Will we keep that I'll believe
It is the river who thanks me
                For our crossing, and not you.
For *waiting for me*, you'll whisper.
                As if I have done you a kindness;
As if my life is not one that began
                Only when we met. As if I had not
Been dead and waiting for you,
                Before.

The attribution reads *"somewheres, some lifetimes ago,"* here a kind of signification that paradoxically marks this story as one that transcends temporalities, eminently connecting past and present.

In another poem—set in Chesapeake, Virginia in 1891—the speaker begins:

Listen. I did not mean to come to you empty
                -Handed. To be yet another who only takes.
My father taught me better than to milk dry
                What I cherish. I want to bring you my fists
Full of wildflowers: buttercups and loosestrife.
                Aster and thistle pure as wind. . . .

Later, the poem makes clear that the "lack" is really an inversion, as it represents the inchoate abundance the speaker intends to create with their beloved. After declaring " . . . darling, I've been an owned thing," they continue:

                . . . —but is beauty enough
Reason to claim what once lived unpossessed?
                Please understand, I had to put them back
In the dirt. I plucked their seeds with my teeth,
                Spat them along the trail. . . .
        . . .
                Think how, when we're sun-pruned and weary,
We'll stroll here, among the wayward blossoms.
                How right—to love in a field of our own making.

The sense of wholeness in Black life is thus symbolized in the generative and sovereign qualities of the field that will spring from and be nurtured by such love. By the final poem in the series, attributed to "*the burning streets of America, 19—,20—,*" the speaker asks:

> And what, my love, but the pasture?
> But the blades refusing to brown
> Beneath this wintered march?
> What else, in this world, can still call
> Itself *living?* Teach me how
> To consider the lilies; all they are
> Because of, all they are despite.
> . . .
> . . . I want, like you, not to seek
> The beast in every bud. To see
> A field of men as yet a field.
> Black though it may be.
> . . .
> . . . Show me what is untouched
> By the godless blue. What here was sown
> With any sense of grace.

As the poem resolves, Love's (and the Field's) restorative energies are still troubled, ever under siege, but the root system of this beloved bond is tenacious as ever, yielding nothing to the "godless blue" who will "stampede on."

> . . . And I am surer, now,
> Of my ugliness, and surer that I love you
> Because you don't try to make me
> Unknow this truth. The sirens,
> The boots, they stampede on. But we alive
> Because of—we alive despite.

Repetition and variation also crop up in Benson's naming of the book's three sections with the same title—"Black Pastoral"—each with particular segments highlighted in bold for different thematic emphases: Black Past, Black As, and Black Pastoral, respectively. I like the way that this wordplay also invites further iterations and connotations—e.g., "Black Past Oral." Going further by means of anagram, the title also yields "Black As Portal"—which I appreciate, too, as another way to muse about Black ontology and a post-liberation future-right-now . . . a linguistic metaphor for blackness as intrinsically multidimensional, fertile, powerful. And, the book's titular poem, "Black Pastoral," underscores endurance and recurrence with the symbol of trees, opening and closing with these lines: "There is a kind of poetry in a turning that leaves / a body redder than before. . . ." and "the trees . . . weep the winter out—the silent sobs a prelude / to the red, not of end, but of moss, of possibility."

There's so much richness in this collection, which I will leave you to now discover, but I should mention that in addition to the ways theme, diction, and ekphrasis echo throughout, there are bold experiments with visible form. These include concrete and contrapuntal poems and a singular example, in "Still Life with Bouquet, Golden Spade (out of frame)," of Benson's invention of the Golden Spade, which "riffs" on Terrance Hayes's Golden Shovel form by embedding a Brooks poem diagonally within its stanzaic structure. With poem after poem, I'm left yearning after the deft expression of certain phrases, images, ideas . . . that I would find such authority in every poem I might ever read hereafter. (See "Epithalamion in the Wake," "Antipastoral: This Green and Pleasant Land," "Rorschach After the Storm," and "Aubade After Earth" among others.) Or, a kind of bewilderment sets in, shaped by the openness or elegiac uncertainty of poems like "On Mars," "Cloud Animals," and "Sweet Field Anemoia," yet I take pleasure in that as well.

Despite all exigencies, *Black Pastoral* ultimately feels like a love story that extends from the past to, borrowing Campt's words, "a temporality that both embraces and exceeds [our] present circumstances." These poems both imagine and recount our ancestors' commitments to one another (and thus the future) and freedom, being often practically and at times mysteriously aided by nature in their perilous journeys. Depicting, as well, our contemporary will to thrive amidst the increasingly tenuous and antagonistic connections of humans to the natural world, Benson reminds us that Black life, love, serenity, and hope continue to hang in the balance.

Sharan Strange
Spelman College
January 2023

Black Pastoral

PROLOGUE
Love Poem in the Black Field

somewheres, some lifetimes ago

I have run so far, so long.
      There is nowhere I haven't been
But here, in this field, a body
      Length from the ragged brink
That gives way to forest.
      I collapsed here, the thin, hard slip
Of me whittled at both ends.
      I want badly to brave this
Aloneness—now, as the hoofbeats swell,
      Like a whip welt, around me
—But I cannot. I weep for you,
      Clutch the hogweed, imagine
It your wrist. Likewise, the stalks
      Refuse to bend, even slightly, inside
My balmy grasp. O my saving
      Grace, my heart's restharrow, mere
Thought of you dams the ploughs
      That would have my head.
When you arrive to pull me up
      From the mud, the salt will crumble
From my eyes; my eyes
      That, for nights, have seen
Nothing, save that cardinal
      North from which the stars beckon;
Those stars that, like you, never fade
      From sight, even in the day
—Blue sky. Then, for weeks,
      Unspeaking, we'll follow their call,

Afraid to make more sound
        Than does a mothling upon her first
And final embrace with the open
        Flame for which she confuses
Caged light. Such silence
        Will we keep that I'll believe
It is the river who thanks me
        For our crossing, and not you.
For *waiting for me*, you'll whisper.
        As if I have done you a kindness;
As if my life is not one that began
        Only when we met. As if I had not
Been dead and waiting for you,
        Before.

I. **Black Past**oral

Epithalamion in the Wake

the Atlantic Ocean, 1619

Now let come two who are chained   5
in hand, in heart. Two who, as dowry,
offer a forever without end. Albatross
and gannet circle on high, pealing
like carillon bells. The white oak gunwale
shredded by rabid brine: your broom to jump.
What sharks do not clamor in the surf
commune under the hull, waiting to adorn
your necks with gum-sprung pearls. The waves
weave an aisle of white horses and foam;
upon it, flowery seagrass floats. Come,
while the billows surge, the froth soft
and warm. While foul minds lie blank.
A body of water is, in the end, but a field
in which you cannot be shackled. Know
yourselves, now, as but souls clothed
in skin, saying *I do* in refusal, as one
above the arched break. The skim waxes.
The altar glistens, starlit. The cowries reel,
throw themselves at your feet. Be now blue
maroons. Unbound by time or tradition,
you took vows a fortnight ago: a sightless swear
uttered in dungeon murk. A promise made
before a thousand sighing silhouettes.
Remember the gaze you learned to trust
absent light, how it returns yours
with equal urgency. How you studied
your betrothed's face with your thumbs—
a love that knows no blind faith is none
at all. A love that knows nothing
but ocean is one they cannot drown.

things tiny enough to fit through Elmina's door of no return

Cape Coast, Ghana, 1482–1814

1 indigo pitted skin
2 pink- tipped fingers
3 wilted iliac basin
4 inlet rippling crystal
5 ilisha herring fin
6 wishes to sink ships
7 iron (ic) crucifix
8 skittering lizard
9 citrine- ringed irises
10 pipistrelle wings
11 titian- tinged ichor
12 sick- sweet stink
13 fetid kiwi rind
14 stilt- thin limbs
15 [1]
16 glimpse of ibis
17 mimicked hymns
18 sliver of light
19 will to live

[1]"invisibility" writ in disappeared ink

Strange Fruit Market

A wild fruit best served fresh and cold,
protruding green blades slice at chained feet.
Cut deep enough, white flesh turns pure gold.

Produce wrenched from its earth-bound mold,
coarse hull scoured with bleach: wash, rinse, repeat.
A wild fruit best served fresh and cold

like skulls beheaded. Crowns tumbled and rolled,
belly skinned, rid of rind that tastes unsweet.
Cut deep enough, white flesh turns pure gold.

Sticky, thick juice runs, blood flow uncontrolled,
brown eyes gouged. Insatiable men need not see to eat
the wild fruit best served fresh and cold.

A stripped core: all that remains to behold,
barren carcass left to rot in sweltering heat.
Cut deep enough, white flesh turns pure gold

to be loaded, bound, shipped 'cross oceans, sold.
Riches reaped from a resource we've yet to deplete:
A wild, strange fruit best served fresh and cold.
Cut deep enough, black flesh turns to gold.

Said the Tobacco to the Hand

Richmond, Virginia, 1705

8

Has your master ever made love
without touching—just dust

carried from legs to air to mouth
on wings almost too gossamer

to lift your body. How do I feel
to the touch: your calluses

like pestle, your palm, mortar.
You leave me desflorado. You,

tender guillotine. My white tongues
crumpled like the sheets

of two damp lovers who've forsaken
the bed they made for a looming dawn.

How often do you dream of running
yourself along a taut spine

that never labored under a name
not her own. What can you tell me

about the ship, its hollow
gut. What kind of dark

it carries: the sweet flesh of free
-range sky, or bitter entrails

even the buzzards would let
the heavens repossess.

When spat up, tooth-ground,
onto cold, foreign earth,

is it best to put down feeble roots
or to refuse to flower at all.

9

Dear Moses Grandy . . . Love, the Great Dismal Swamp

It was the dense, tangled hostility of the [Great Dismal] swamp and its enormous size
that enabled hundreds, and perhaps thousands, of escaped slaves to live here in freedom.
—Smithsonian Magazine, 2016

Here, among snakes, bears and panthers . . . I felt to myself so light, that I almost
thought I could fly. . . I then thought I would not have left the place to go to heaven.
—Captain Moses Grandy, 1843

I send men swarms of insects in the shape of your ghost.
They are not wrong to think me haunted, possessed as I am
by spirits exhumed from bodies left strewn in my wake. I trick
them into thinking me God, but to them I am Eden, wicked

paradise of poison, fruit and beasts. I steep sweat from acrid
flesh, sip it in pinpricks with the tongues of jewel-toned bees.
I spill their blood in your name. When it seeps into my murk, I turn
a rich maroon hue, and I remember you fondly, longing

for nights when there was nothing but you and me, twilight's ichor
and wind quivering in my reeds—a southern serenade. I hope
you knew I heard the song of your silence, your heartbeat
camouflaged in the thrumming pulse of mine. Now, they smelt

molten asphalt into my arteries, litter the air with my ashes. I watch
myself burn and search for your face in the flames. I knew you
then as amalgam of marsh and man, sometimes just tar-black
beads sunk into star-white glow—your eyes glinting in the glass

of my stillness. Under the cover of dusk, you snuck nips of raw
honeysuckle, lugged saw-shorn Juniper trunks through my mud.
Like your namesake, you made many waters from my one,
and like the Red Sea, I opened—bared my soul to your people,

and closed to your tormentors. I cherish the sacred pleasure
of being parted by your hands. I ache for the long-ago days
when your vessel's crest gently unzipped my quiet mire
like the waning sun ripples liquid along the horizon's serrated blade.

You told me then that you would not have left me for Heaven itself,
so I drag them through the Hell they wanted me to be for you.

Love Poem in the Black Field

Fayette County, Tennessee, 1861

12

Because I saw you, alone, your broad body slicing
           The thick fat of night. I shouldn't have been able
To make you out, but I know your shadow, his dance.
           Because you can see in the dark like I can, eyes used
To lack of light, keen as those of the livestock they claim
           Are our kin. Because you name them all, even the cattle:
Jeremiah, Temperance, Rebel. Because you look
           At the animals like you look at all the living and look at me
Like molasses in your hand. You freed that dying cow—
           You believe a life is worth more than her milk.
You lead her into the woods, walked until she wasn't
           Afraid of what was beyond this land, and I was terrified
To rest, to leave you in that heavy fog. Because you returned
           And I praised the Lord, and that joy roils
Like guilt in my gut. Because when they beat you wet
           I heaved, and when I wailed for you, you wiped my cheek.
Because you know fear; because you know how to live anyway.

Boll Weevil's Theodicy

A white southerner told of hearing a black man from Georgia singing while working on a road construction project in North Carolina. The words of the song were simple, almost like a nursery rhyme:

> Boll weevil here, boll weevil there,
> boll weevil everywhere;
> Oh, Lordy, ain't I glad!

What caught the white man's attention and disturbed him was that the black man seemed genuinely glad. There was, he said, 'a note of genuine gladness, almost of exultation in the voice singing it, not unlike the note one hears between lines in the Old Testament songs of Jews triumphing over the downfall of their enemies. It seemed a song of emancipation.'

—from "The Strange Affair of the Boll Weevil:
The Pest as Liberator" by Dr. Arvarh E. Strickland

Wilmington, North Carolina, 1922

Don't evil exist to remind men of their weakness?
Didn't I dent the Devil's chin, gnaw them holes in his pockets?
And wasn't I summoned to make white men believe

that though they may own land, they live at Your mercy?
Didn't I bend stubborn knees, twist necks towards a new green
god? Remind evil men how their weak existence

can be crushed to pulp under Your heaven-high boot?
Wasn't it pestilence, six-legged blackness smotherin' all
the white sky, that first made men into believers?

Or was it Moses himself, burnin' bushes from the inside—
and if so, ain't I the flame? Or the serpent, fearsome mark
of evil, and so, of your existence? To remind men of their weakness,

didn't I, a wretched li'l thing, pen my own Exodus, the Mississippi
my Red Sea? Hitch squalls upriver and rain down like blessings,
like white manna? God on high, what else can I believe

now, as I lay on my back, dying, as all we evils do?
What is my gluttony if not proof that You, my Lord,
are good? And who better to remind evil of its weaknesses
than a hell-sent pest even white men believe has none?

Elders Speak of the Windchimes

that quivered in the maples, the poplars, the hollowed pipes, their coppered shine in the gloaming, some notched with patterns as if by potter's curved blade, some filled to the mouth with birdseed and monkshood, as if to lure the crows and hornets and citrus swallowtails— and so they came, pitch-hued and thick as locusts—

some intoned a song that followed elders everywhere: on the smoked-out bus, in the old vine-mangled lean-to, past the corner store, resounding through the sundown valleys, through the tobacco leaves, a sour sound, like the ringing in your teeth after the first bite of an underripe nectarine, it became the score of their dreams, that chimesong;

chimes made of bloodwet Stone Mountain clay and kiln-fired Gullah mud, chimes those icy gales withered to bone, chimes that sung all alone without other chimes to strike, to crack their sorrow against, and louder, still, than the solo chimes, were the chimes that had others alongside them, others with whom to lift that flickering din heavenward: that soprano trill that could be heard over the midnight crickets, over even the thunderous Sunday organs, over the caterwauling sinnermen, over the rejoicing children of God.

Etymology of Mercy

miséricorde: French for 'mercy.' also a knife
wielded to usher suffering knights into death;
sometimes, it means 'forgiveness,' as in, 'I
forgive your fall by tying stones to your feet
mid-descent.' a clement blade brandished
also against enemies, as in, 'allow my mercy
to free you from this life wasted on the futility
of stabbing at mine.' so surgical, this mercy
that finds the gaps in a corset of ivory parentheses,
to breach the aortic dam. tenderly, I fold
your palm around the gilded hilt, smother it
with my own. fingers, like tongues, plunge—
a French mercy kiss. *Lord have mercy* says my grandma
when we hear the rigored hiss of a still-warm
body forgiven into frigid ground; sizzling, fissured
like molten gold drowned in a pail of water.
I repeat this prayer, the same God answers,
but He mouths *mercy* with maroon lips, speaks
the creole of the first to carve forgiveness
into impinging skin, to take mercy into their own
sugarbit grip.

                    for the bladesmiths who mass-smelt
weapons from scrap-metalled men: mercy. I insist
you taste the amnestied brass you forge. to you dead
-eyes who snipe anything black enough to be *shadow*,
I give the meticulous mercy the gin gave heads
of cotton in offering a clean break. mercy, mercy me.
merci: French for 'thank you.' to the architects
of our darkness, in the absence of a misericorde,
I present my silken fists in gratitude. may my hands,
damp with starshine, grace the supple clay
of your neck into a spindled flute. oh, how you'll sing

of my bone-whet caress, how kindly I wring
rings of mercy into your throat. you
who whittled the cross into a crude shiv—I christen
forgiven. baptize breathless over, and over,
and again. you who sate your crops with flesh
-drawn rain, I wish nothing but miseri
-corde. *merci*, I thank you. for all the times
you heaped upon us a generous mercy
we had done nothing to deserve.

Love Poem in the Black Field

Chesapeake, Virginia, 1891

Listen. I did not mean to come to you empty
      -Handed. To be yet another who only takes.
My father taught me better than to milk dry
      What I cherish. I want to bring you my fists
Full of wildflowers: buttercups and loosestrife.
      Aster and thistle pure as wind. I paid the man
At the riverbank—his cedarwood cart splintered
      By the brackish spray, his nailbeds stained
A deep blue that fades, like shoreline, into tan.
      I bought you a lush posy to hold
While we watch schooners troll the swamp.
      But darling, I've been an owned thing.
I've been the orphan calf, baying; been the birth
      -Damp hay cut and baled a few days before.
I know we keep livestock for meat and hides,
      Hens for their eggs—but is beauty enough
Reason to claim what once lived unpossessed?
      Please understand, I had to put them back
In the dirt. I plucked their seeds with my teeth,
      Spat them along the trail. Felt each one crush
Under the stone of my heel as I walked here, to you.
      I know I must sound mad. I hope I'm the kind
Of mad that makes you feel most whole.
      Think how, when we're sun-pruned and weary,
We'll stroll here, among the wayward blossoms.
      How right—to love in a field of our own making.

Cruel Ripening

To crush a summer thing into sweet gore—
        such field trip bliss, an indulgent spoil of war. We're told

to amputate any bad berries we find, to keep sickness
        from spreading through the patch. We're too young to respect

what even the plants themselves have left for dead.
        We skip bulbs like bang snaps at each others' ankles,

our ammo spangled with slimy seeds, with mold gray
        as permafrost. Laughing, we make magazines of plastic baskets

loaded with produce one sun from fermenting into moon
        -shine. Red splashes off jeans, our soles repatriate the wrung-out

mush to the dirt. When struck center mass, we fall into the waist
        -wide rows, let the ultraviolet embalm us into hot specimens.

Aphids hover, unable to resist what, to them, is sap-rich and stiff.
        We, adolescent in this patch, begin to sense what sprouts sour

around us—but we haven't yet grown beyond ignorance
        of what such a scene may bode. If there are any clouds overhead

that day, I don't notice. But I do note the scored plot
        of my palm; its dark brown verso, in the sun turning darker,

as it begs questions of this land, its history, my play
        upon it. This hand: made to pick in heat, made to find sugar

in low places. We, more than the blunt-toothed leaves,
        are so very green. And I, alone in my own way, greener still.

Our limbs windless, crimson wounds flower like carnations
              on our chests. Magenta juice dyes our smiles. Our sweaty bodies

betray the cruelty of ripening. What a sight we must be
              to passing traffic. What a sight I am

to those watching from earlier fields.

II. **Black** P**as**toral

Theodicy on My Blackness

To know the tiger is to know God
has claws the width of her stripes.
The first tiger, born unpatterned,
did not go lightly into her own mauling,
appreciating, from then on, the agony
she need inflict to eat, to survive.
The centipede took an extra foot
for every step its venom might deny.
The lizard plucked his legs from the snake
in exchange for becoming her prey. Eve
bit the apple, and Adam, having watched,
swallowed the remainder. It lodged
whole in all his sons' throats. Even He
created a son, a world, all to know
any kind of lasting suffering. Wearied
after eons of cosmic perfection—
as if loneliness, boiled down to its core,
were truly a pressing want for pain.
You understand, by now, that this life
is one of impossible choices; that His fair
does not match our own. That the apparent
spotless are simply less willing
to be reminded of some original
sin. I know who I was before
I took this body. Before His asking
what color skin in which I'd like to wash
my soul. And when I chose, I remember
His allowing me the dignity
of not asking if I was sure.

Antipastoral

This Green and Pleasant Land

I have no wonder left for petrichor.

No heart to marvel at osmanthus,
sumac. My eye idles in the grass
of your sprawling country
-scapes, glazed with matte patina.

In your pristine pastoral, God
lords above a lea of moaning cattle.
If men walk here, none notice the irony
of His painting the cows
both black and white at once.

But I am meant to swoon
at the sight of water
-lilies, of quail pecking
at blackberries the same way
boar revel in the lush
throat of a kill.

Never mind the fireflies
that have all but gone.

Never mind who once blistered
on this *green and pleasant land*.

There's nothing you can tell me about beauty.

About what glory languishes
untended, blooming mutinous
despite all morass and blur.

So if I must admire the magpies,
their morbid halo, you will
look first, unflinching,
at what festers in the brush:

the saltating maggots, the feasting
butterflies; their dripping
wings.

Love Poem in the Black Field

Parchman Farm Chain Gang, Sunflower County Mississippi, 1911

How long since my left foot has known a day
          It did not spend drug along by your right? Since the first
Rust-iron rattlers made fields of cattails kneel, fronds
          Curdling like browlines in brutal heat? I forget
My name, its sins, when I march behind you. I know nothing
          Of before. Nothing but your nape, its tributary of creases;
But your gait, pressing smooth miles of streetside weeds.
          What else can a lonesome roadboy do but look
At the one to his front: you, with keloid scars inside
          Even your ears, you with long lashes that, when blinked,
Seem heavier than these chains, all the men they carry.
          What I wouldn't give to see your eyes open again
After that brief, merciful closing. What I don't have
          To give. What I know, if I did, I would.

Self-Portrait as Oil Spill

In the brief still, I *appear* within   a sickening iridescence.
My skin muck-pocked like *a* **Pollock.**   Fish bubble up like zits, **heads**
bloated, leaking.   Waves of rot waft into the air,   the dead*sweet*
eau de parfum   of never-hatched eggs   licks my neck—the **smell** of sulfuric
neglect, of ante-life   shriveled *on* the vine. A duck's tailing, *V-shaped* wake   furrows
my brow. The hapless **bird looks**   nothing like the **downy ones** in Dawn
commercials—cute,   and **thus**, worth saving   with **lathered**, neon blue savon.
Pitiful, yet unpitied,   a once honking bellow   now a choked bark.   Her sun-bright
eyes set into midnight,   left leg cuffed by congealed sludge,   she spirals.
So, too, do I **swim** around   nothing but myself. I   **rise** to survey the whole
of **the inlet, now** stippled   at the **edges**, surface puckered *like* chapped lips
shedding **dried-out** pigment. Then   **fingers unfurl** like **kudzu** around my neck,
dunking my head,   pulling **me into a kiss with my** own dark simile.   Filth warps
the red hyacinth   buds of my **lungs that burn bloody**   with each futile gasp;
my own ecosystem   in *beta decay.* **I know** now   what the drowning see
just before   they drift stagnant: **nothing but oil**,   even in the cleanest   of seas.
Just as stars start to spark   in the   **sky of my** dying, the grip   relents, satisfied
with its **vicious** baptism.   I can't tell   **you**   what was reborn   within me, **but I am**
certain of what expired: **everything but the white**   of my eyes and **teeth**.
I hear footsteps   **retreating**   **into horizon behind me and whip** my head around, **hoping**
to find the face   of the **one who has tried to send my being**   into the past tense.
My *lashes* drunk   **with greasy mascara, I see only shadow.**   A barge rolls by
and *in my* frantic   **waving for help, I catch a glimpse** of   my own hand,
palms black   **as all that ever was, knuckles sticky**   with crude guilt.
I wipe   **my face, turn back to the spill in**   disbelief.
What   **had I expected to see except**   myself?

How to Run Away

It is June, the wheat has been cut and enslaved farm boys are availing
themselves of an old privilege granted them at harvest time of taking
any rabbits they are lucky enough to capture in the stubble.

You want the first stone
big and slow, with the heavy smack
of a well pail on still water.
This will scatter them, make long
ears stretch and flatten like a back
before a leather braid.

     A warning
shot they think they can outrun.
Guide your target with the light
pebbles you toss to flush them out. Aim
where their scampering will bend the grass
next—a hand held over a stove learns fast
where it's hot. The flame must learn, too.
Then go silent.

     A running animal
is most vulnerable when it thinks
it has just then, at that moment,
escaped. Watch for the exhale,
how its starved flank deflates with relief
as it will in your boiling water.
Here's my sharpest stone: when thrown,
with any luck, it will be sticky
from before.

Move quick. Take
no pride in chasing down what limps.
Don't forget to pray. They say God
chooses what grasses to let the scythe
lower, that all we need to be is strong
enough when the time comes
to swing the blade. To the hare,
you God. You say what gets cut when.

Anti-Elegy for the Trees

How tired I've grown of the trees   their weeping
boughs, the musty slop of the leaves   they discard, wanton, wet

on the ground   their seedy fruit ripened into rancor
their stagnation that passes   for something like humility

their relentless decay   into barely mortared shrapnel
duned under mossed earth   until a storm presses

the full brunt of its heel   how they made of me a wary child
who knew to dread a hurricane   mostly for what the trees could do

as it raged, how they seem to lean   into splintering fragility
lean   up against our human softness

What I know of indignity   I unearthed in my father's black
eyes   when Isabel's kicking gusts snapped that terrible White

Oak   The grandest tree I knew, it held the roots
of his pride, which drew into early winter   as he was forced to crawl

calloused hand over foot   over the downed tree's berth, through split
branches and clumped burrs   just to get to work that day, crushing

what remained   of robins' and squirrels' thatched dens—
evidence of some urge that possesses wildlife   to nest

in the ficklest of outgrowths   Though who am I to judge
another's home, knowing myself   what it is to shelter

in something bound for ash

\\\

Procyon lotor; Vulpes vulpes; Ursus americanus   the words I didn't have then
for what the other bankers must have thought   of my father, his skin

scratched and slick with struggle   The animal they cast of him
in the flimsy silence   of glances—worse, of looking

away. The nerve of them   those damned trees, to, lie
lifeless, as if they understand what we never could   As if so evolved

beyond any foolish hope   that it's possible to rise again after so brutal
a culling, that there is anything to do in that wake   but allow oneself

to be cleared away,   in whatever manner most pleases the upright
Who are we to deny the carpenter his craft?   the trees ask, mocking

How they loom over us   even the long-petrified
in this righteous better knowing

Yes, it's true, we need them   and I'll concede their beauty, but how I tire, too, and sooner still
of beauty—especially the kind we understand   as needed—

the kind that looks most fantastic in relief   as dark absence framing a low hanging
sun, and is so defined by its inverse   by what can be marked as *ugly*, or sorrier

ordinary

\\\\\

Look, I can't make sense   of this scabbed grudge
Thorns nestled in the sweetness   of my throat

stick me at the thought   of his dirty shirt, of that day I fell
out of my beloved playground Maple   Bark grating my stomach

I slid, in sap-slow agony   onto the sand that spat like gunpowder
under my shoes, my hands hot with betrayal   My blouse relieved of its pearl buttons

How dare that tree not hold me   as had its kind so many of mine before?
My arms not taut, not braided twine   and so not rope enough?

Please, excuse my coarse tone   my manners more pitiful than strewn limbs
I've tried to swear off speaking ill of the dead   (I could argue

for the gray area of the dying)   though that promise means nothing
except this: I'll bite my tongue   only when the last tre blackens

And even then, so many will grieve   their burning
whereas any tears welled   in the aftermath of our fires, of all those

burnings   were pulled from onlookers' ducts
merely by the sting of smoke   Oh trees, how I fear you

haven't taught me much   more than the difference
between weeping   and watering eyes

Rorschach After the Storm

                                                                        after Julie Mehretu

36

charred ruins
of switchgrass fields &
cane dripping
with horseflies
& the cinders slithering
high & swarming
locusts' flight paths   and/or
filigreed into metal—

the passerines
descended at last
diving horizontal
into the glass, the glass
& bones
breaking & who
turned their world
on its side—

cheeks' worth
of spit-tin snuff flung
up like paint on
the ghost of a wall—
                    //
the heavens crumbled
overhead, falling, nova
-first & didn't you know
a lot of stars are made
of lead—

the eyes, the *eyes* &
the black-eyed
susans' disk
florets crowded one right
up on the next, flat
to flat edge, never
to aspirate what hasn't
already been
inside another—

sound of cracker—oil
-dyed and copper-plated
onto air like the black back
of throats, of open
mouths, the water, debris   or & and/or
dead in the flood

& the shingles plunging
from roofs to wet
gloom, the roofs atop
which they screamed, the
screams
black, and so un—

& under it all, the city
it all's all city
don't you understand
it's all Damascus, its' all Ninth Ward
all dammed, until it is—

Black Pastoral

There is a kind of poetry in a turning that leaves
a body redder than before. Golden drupes ripen,
orchards flush rouge. Sweetness curls the blades
of leaves that once sprouted green. Fall confetti rains
red herrings in pretend surrender: showers of bleeding
white flags. Yes, even the trees play possum
when a cold force looms larger than they. They freeze,
mine stone from wood, statue themselves like deer.
Enter the fledgling buck. See him, just barely: a tawny smudge
blinking back at you through the landscape's static.
His molting crown: one shredded antler a tree in its own
visceral autumn, the other a felled trunk at rest
in the ashen grass. *Enter the Black boy.* See his boots leave
little coffin-prints in the ground—what lingers in the foam
of his wake. They stand together, this boy, this deer,
each a lone solstice removed from fawnhood, from his spring
-pink and summer-blushed self, the memories of whom live
only in the glossy black of the other's eyes. They reminisce
for a moment in unblinking silence. Then, see
the boy's tiny hands, dotted with birch-knot knuckles, his womb
-smooth palms split along umber fault lines, as they meet
to cradle the lost horn and turn it upright in the frost,
making sapling of skeleton. Now hear a distant whistling,
a herd of cocked rods dragging like fingernails over the shivering
ground, its goosebumped skin. See our subjects assume the position
of hibernation, of stagnant and threatless sleep, praying
they will awaken when the white recedes. They learned,
in leaving the red of their mothers, the danger of hound
-snouted men, who, upon cornering a creature dark
with life, ponder the taste of metal-peppered flesh.
They know to freeze, to still their limbs, wait for the melt,
for the trees to weep the winter out—the silent sobs a prelude
to the red, not of end, but of moss. Of possibility.

Crown Shyness

There are some trees—the black mangrove, the longleaf pine— that cannot bear the loneliness of touch. Or, perhaps, of having been, and no longer being, touched: the difference between loving someone, that warmth, that shared light, and what memory of them remains too close to be *past.* I was wrong not to ask if you wanted me. You never said more than you needed to. Had to. But there was something like a canopy, though fractured, between us, that seemed to gently shade what had mushroomed down below. Enough for lichen to spread, soften. Whatever was there was delicate: an orb weaver's silk, an evening bat's purr. My only regret is that we're still too young for regret. But what could we have done, then, except be by ourselves, together.

Aubade After Earth

we wake only to growing
bristles of heat. more undark
-ness than ante-light. no chirping
trills to jumble the senses,
to arrythmia night's violet
hum. no cygnets to rain
trumpet sobs on tattered
rooftops. no rain. no roofs.

I miss the birds.

but it's truer that you ache
for their song. the score that lured
seeds of luster into bloom.
we haven't been gone long
enough to miss a thing more
than what it made for us. here,
we radiate a platinum sheen

—yet, in the smallest of mercies,
we know ourselves, still,
as Black. I fled
just before the brimstone,
left the world to salt
herself over.

I wonder what still lives
among the grains.

I would ask in earnest, but even if I had
a spare dove, how cruel
to send it searching for a lone
green star in the sparse constellation
of what once was forest.
of what was, once.

that last night under the trees, you
plucked a leaf from my hair,
pressed it against my cheek.
I threaded pine straw
through the back and forth
of its ribboned blade,
the damp spire dyed
my fingertips the bronze
of fresh regret.

sometimes I sleep
with it behind my ear, the swell
of your pulse still breaking
perfect as its sinus wave.

a few crooked notes—that's all I had
to offer in return. all I have sung since.
it's just as well that I leave
my voice to make shelter
of your mind—somewhere
it might survive.

what has apocalypse taught us
but how to love
unwholly?

Where do you go in the morning?

you feel me lying
here, folded into the back
and forth of you, but know I'm lost
in those woods. you dread
the hour when my eyes glacier,
just before the demiblue thaws
their whites. how long can we pretend
this turn toward Earth's still
-lit wick brings the same warmth
as dawn, that fuming glow
could ever kiss with the soft lips
of sunning sky?

what new life can there be
without forgetting
those given over
to flame?

I sigh,
Nowhere. . .

and crumble the quiet,
confirm you have not dreamt
my breath's susurrus on the plain
of your nape: a wind that passes
for honesty. for what
I still know of it.

Still Life with Unidentified Flora

I.

The flowers dying in the vase, the black-eyed susans
and lavender, especially, refuse my unrefined pity, sorry
in its own right. My stares filter through their dry wisps
and catch on the tree in the yard, the one with the severed
branch dangling, the dead limb almost as long and full as a boy
some would call a man.

I am ashamed that I do not know from which kind of tree
my mind has just hung that body. This memory is not
a memory of a boy who was never a boy, but a branch
the tree will carry until it cannot. The tree would be right not to
accept my shame as an apology.

II.

Above the head-high arm of the jockey
on the flowers' vase, a whip stretches, curving subtly
in the shadow-dimmed porcelain. I spare the horse my sadness
at the impending sting of leather on his brown flank—

the flowers have taken that sorrow as their own. I am reminded
again of what I am inventing: the pitcher is black and white;
so, too, the horse and his rider. Where else
have I found color where it never grew?

III.

The flowers that, for what little I know, could be tickseed
and Russian sage, stand firm when I offer one last apology, a pitcher
of fresh water. And I consider this, how thin an offering of life
when made under the wrong name, transparent as condensation on a pane
through which I see another tree, its even smaller boy.

I can no less forgive my mind than can a saw forgive its blade
on behalf of what it has unmade. The drops of water
on the glass face of the door run fast toward the ground.
The limb is cut from the tree's body. The flowers,
at last, shudder and bow.

Love Poem in the Black Field

Caroline County, Virginia, 1954

for Mildred and Richard

The darkness we need is possible only in myth.
       We, like the titans, are almost certainly too much;
Us laid flat on my quilt, this antebellum tapestry
       Beneath our backs, our heaving ribs pressing valleys
Into the June bugs' grass. And it is theirs, this grass,
       Because it was theirs first. I'm afraid, more than you
Can fathom, that we will die if we touch. If we so much as
       Look. So do what you can with the glancing, gaze trained,
Instead, on the stars under whom we bask; tranquil, without fear
       Of joining them in their hanging. Many pasts have made me
Their captive. I was theirs first, long before I was mine.
       For now, we wait out the setting: the red, the orange,
The melting heavens. Anticipate that precious absence
       Of light. I tell you *a vivid sunset means the world
Below is one day closer to dead*, and you know I mean *beauty
       Is never just that; is not to be trusted.* I trust myself, somehow,
Less. I wish this thing I hold for you was plain, expected.
       A pale blue vein cradled nightly in a warm, black grasp.
You say *the moon gives off no glow of its own, merely reflecting
       What the sun has to spare.* And I understand our love
Is nothing without that sun under whose glare it will surely
       burn. *Yes*, I say, *how beautiful*; and we would be.
How beautifully close to dead.

III. Black Pastoral

Still Life with Bouquet, Golden Spade (out of frame)

I paint flowers so they will not die.
—Frida Kahlo

47

we be bouquets, be green, leaves
  ethereal, be wildweeds, be *lamb's-quarter*, be *day*
-*flowers'* cool blue, be hue busting
  up bleak blur. we *evening primrose, morning*
  glory, and *larkspur*, left-bent like sunlight
  thru hickory shagbark, schooled in all the ways
  of soil, the ways of lowdirt. we the garden and the gold
-en spade used to till. we the tiny lurking mantis
veiled in verdure, praying under-blade. lately it seems
    all there is to do is wait. and wait we will. we out
        -will winter, bide out the gnaw of blight strikes, we outroot
          the storm's walled eye, our spine-stems straight, sepals
              unsnapped, petals parted but unshed. we hardy *anthurium*,
                    philodendron, monstera, we sing silky with cordiform
                        tongues sweating rosin, we bleed. we blood. we
                        be bloodied as thorns, we be blushed as *trumpet*
                        lily, as *Damask rose*. things of beauty—we.
                        we the bolls survived the gin, we the clouds
                        in our own sky, the birds too. we be *dandelion*,
                        be *red jasmine*, be jazz. we flush
                        just once, like *sweet four o' clock* in June, buds
                        unfist for a foreday's bloom. we hear
                        sorry swoons: "how lovely. how quick they die. Die
                                so soon."

Baptism with Chiaroscuro

after a black-and-white photograph of four men
baptizing a woman in a neighborhood retention pond

As a child, I was convinced that people died
when they were baptized. That air could be
bottled inside submersed lungs for safe-
keeping, that a covered, cold body was not
necessarily wet with death—these truths
stretched beyond the scope of what my mind
could conjure. All I truly knew of this
holy withholding of breath was learned
from photographs like this one. Just look
at the way everything in it cries: the tilted
trees in the distance, weeping viscous
sweetness from their stems; the house
in the background, its upstairs windows
propped awake like a pair of eyes heavy
with the prelude to a damp blink;
the mirrored telephone poles framing
the landscape, twisted awry with tears.
I imagine they angled this way on purpose,
that they corkscrewed into the soil
to transform themselves from common
stakes into crucifixes, from mere objects
into symbols. And then there are the men
dressed like pallbearers who abandoned
their suit-jackets shoreside. But a life
developed in tender Blackness, like old-
school film, trains the eyes to look for sound.
So I know that the liquid ripples do more
than simply show that people have waded into
the water—they sing it. A body is sometimes one

made of water, sometimes of flesh—no matter
the form, it is always haunted by this thing
we hear as *voice*. There are only three
differences between a funeral and a baptism.
One: the casket's state of matter. Two: whether
the drowning opens or closes the ritual.
Three: the tempo at which the spirituals
are hummed. Absent sound or motion, grief
is nearly indistinguishable from joy.
They are complementary emotions, most
potent when felt in tandem, like the chiaroscuro
of the black gown beneath the white hood,
the Black hand cradling the head tucked
into the white bonnet, the white linen draped
over the entirety of a reborn Black body.

Hotbeds in Norfolk, Virginia

It's nothing to be woken by the hammering
racket of collapse. To bathe with tap
drip the tint of hands' sun sides. Life
among ruins means something is falling
at all times. Means knowing how long I have
to get out from under a spreading shadow.

Today, they flattened the house across the street
into memory—siding panels rotting like rinds
in the yard's clovers and crabgrass. It's constant,
the vinyl harvest: red, yellow, pink—all stripped
to the same blanched flesh. To make a space
more enticing, they say. But I was fed
on sweetness sprung up from dirt, and nobody
skins an apple they intend to candy.

O'Hara wrote, once, about Norfolk.
Said to have exercised here—blown
breath into air, here—is to have *been to bed
with a Nigra* and what a way to admit knowing
a place only by the way it looks from above,
when on top of it, moving in and out of it at will.

Last week, they erased the turquoise house,
its kitchen where I learned not to play around
the hot stove, where I earned scars
the one in my bed grazes with lips
brown like water, like mine.

Someone silenced the rocks we kicked
down the blacktop, their scrapes filling the gaps
in conversation. Someone keeps sticking the same
scribbled-on slips between my locked door

and its frame. Someone sprayed the big weed
that planted itself in the fractured concrete
before we could even bend our tongues
to dub it *flower*. Soon, all the wrong green
will be brought to wilt.

Truth is, there are many Norfolks full
of our deep hotbeds, our colorful plots. It's nothing
to pass one while driving, to speed up at the first
sign of us: the rubbled lot of a First, or Second
or Seventh Baptist Church, for instance—
the black dust of its crumbling
never allowed to settle. And so you roll
your windows up, tighten your hold
on your breath.

Game Theory

Men will talk of the wolves,
the gray wrath they're said
to have wrought upon the pale
-bellied elk, upon the ranchers,
their sheep and cattle, the live

-stock the ranchers breed,
and so solely own
the right to slaughter. Of course,
men will talk of the land
the wild dogs have overrun,

the profusion of dandelions, now
with fewer hare to, at the least,
pare the ragged yellow
heads, keeping the verdance
uniform, acceptable.

Yes, even the weeds
will be spoken of, if not for.
No one will mention the men
themselves: men raised to lay waste
what seems to walk too close

to the earth. Men whose fathers took
others' lower gait as proof that the sky,
if not God himself, belonged
to their kind. Even the failing men
whose arthritic fingers warp

around the memory of their first
trigger pull, its sick recoil.
Men who have long lost
the taste for hare and elk,
for even the wolves,

and so supplement their hunt
in denser forests. Men like
the one that night at the highway
gas station—forced in the present
season to settle for culling

(as evidenced by the grille
-scored carcass in his cargo bed)
only through chance brushes
with nature—who spoke his seething
spit at my feet, the road

-kill having been ample whet.
In saying 'no one' earlier
I told something of a half-truth:
many have condemned the exploits
of these men—but other throats

are thought not to speak
for God, and so may as well be those
of wolves. But for the grace of these whispers
—not entirely unlike guttural howls
warning of the inevitable white

moon—did I go into that dark, noticing
the man perched in his four-wheel
drive treestand, thinking
it best to ignore him, taking
the calculated risk of leaving

my younger brother, the bigger game
of us two, in the car to keep
watch as I went inside to pay.
But for the cover of the chrome
canopy, my brother's steady eyes tinged gold

beneath its buzzing lights—the lights,
which made for a poor repellent,
but just enough of one
that this encounter was nothing
worth speaking of.

A Certain Sickness

Maybe I carry animals in my pockets.
And where you imagine I've tucked a barrel's nose,
lies instead the huffing muzzle of a beast
untroubled by my fleshwarm dark. A hunger I thumb
through all of taxonomy to identify: fanged
as a piranha, madder than an abandoned cub. When I disappear
my fists into those twin wilds, they reemerge
claw-mauled and oozing. How delicious, this agony
like pressing a bruise to deeper blue and branding it *night*.
Allow me, if nothing else, a moment to lap at what leaks.
I have a certain sickness that makes me love
my freshest stripes, and maybe I'm proudest of this
red touch. Of the way no one leaves my embrace
with a shirt white as it was when I first held them.
My sternum, itself a pocket; my clavicles, threadbare seams.
My gasp catches soft as lint in thick hair. When I die,
I hope to leave behind—more than an unleaded chest—
a viscid stain, its brassy wax. Maybe all I need
is to know men won't walk away from me clean.

Still Life with Tulip as Grenade

Each tulip petal is blanketed by its own personal imposter.
        A doppelgänger sepal giving its finest impression of bloom.
Eremurus, Phalaenopsis, Hellebore—all haloed at the base

        by wreaths of colorful leaves. We ourselves are not above playing
at majesty when it suits us, when it can be slipped smoothly out of
        like a dagger from a too-loose sheath. Now, let the scene drain

to grisaille: a wrought iron bench; a dull pair of pupils leering
        through a Queen Anne's Lace chalet; the once arabesque garden
now more pastiche of peeling stones, suspended; the tulips still

        longing to know the blushed petal of a rabbit's tongue, the sound
embrace of sinew; the boy, in monochrome an altered hue, but Black
        all the same; his hand cradling a single grey head—a grenade

with only whistle where the pin of green stem used to be.
        Let's say we're grateful that gunmetal black tulips are rare,
that the powder emptied from pistils onto his skin

        was only pollen. No—let's not say *thank you*. We can exhale
this snatched gasp corroding our lungs without pretending
        it's anything more than sick relief. Think, now, of the boy

in the courtroom, seated at a table his eyes have not yet grown to meet,
        coloring in the scene once more. His fingers, dirt brown, raking
back and forth across the page. Think of the flowers left

        in the ground, feigning dead silence, wondering what to do
about the imagined problem of Black boys who find beauty
        in all the wrong places.

On Mars

i. 57

I was never much   one for astronomy   My basic grasp   of the universe and its terrifying
contents satisfied me   most of my life. Pluto was a planet   then wasn't, then was again. I think   I
didn't go outside   to witness the eclipse because I've spent   too many moons waiting
for obstacles to pass between my world   and its light, for celestial corpses   to align. To deem them
bodies   implies life and humans   have long known   Earth only as a ghost

//

But when I see that water   has been found on Mars, I feel   a knot that my heart   urges my tongue
to curl into   hope. I see life, blossoming   bundles of cells that compose   bodies instead of
confining   them. I see babies'   tiny feet splashing in puddles
from which their very existence sprung   I see water on Mars   and know my children
must never call home   by any other name

Our backyard awash in desert   rust, we'll fashion palaces from red   sand, all the while sipping tea
sweetened with spoonfuls   of stardust. When winter rains   turn craters into ponds, we'll skate
atop their frosted faces   and in summer laze   in their pooled relief   from the heat The natal
knowledge   of how to swim   having never fled   a single child's mind

//

hey'll have a galaxy   of nebulae to nightly gaze   upon, hair bathed in cool   slate absent white-hot sun   Gravity an alien bondage   they'll play ball   palm entire planets, bound through the asteroid belt, swing   from Saturn's rings with their fingertips   Astral amphibians, they'll breathe purified pink sky through their skin   Not a single gasp   will escape their grip

On Mars there are no guns   What good are bullets   that can be batted down   like balloons
bleeding air?   My children will thrive   they'll climb mountains only   to leap fearless   from the
peaks   and drift back to Mars   serene like leaves   in a crisp autumn breeze   colorful and bright
and beautiful and whole   They will have all   of outer space to reach
their true peaks and drift   back to me. Colorful, bright, beautiful   whole

Cloud Animals

We're driving—no, I'm driving—and you've left me
for the woods. Leaned back, silvered nape kissing

the top of your shoulders, you grab my free hand
to point with it, as if the hand's sole purpose is to lead

the eye to sight. You grin. *Tell me you don't see a bear.*
My foot weighs down the brake. The stoplight

is red, so I join you among the trees that could pass,
perhaps to a younger eye, for clouds. We search

for animals: a squirrel in a monkey's gentle fist;
a fish, just leapt from a fragile creek; the back

of a fox's head. You say, *Can't you just imagine*
that bird flying through the sky? Yes, I say.

If only it were real, your forest of stumbling cubs
and buds yawning the mist from their lips. And you

forever in it. Just out of your view, a doe hangs,
suspended. The light seems redder now. I tell you

to look at the swan, its folded neck. A car backfires.
You blink. The doe is no more. It's my fault.

More than death, I fear its impending: a heavy grey
blanket dragged slow over all our heads.

You're not mine to wish gone, yet I do wish for that
blue nothingness to arise where there remain

only pale wisps broken up by planes and wind and life.
How to tell someone: I want *after* for you.

The light changes, drains the green
from the trees that wither under the weak sun

of your memory. My foot loses its lead.
Your hand loses my hand to the turning wheel.

No. 2 (No. 7 and No. 2): oil on canvas: Mark Rothko: 1951

64
The first breath is always the rawest. This can't
be helped. All the sillage of the preceding one—

the motor exhaust, the taste, metallic like fingers
after clutching old change, of blood, the ragged

desperation—it's all still there. Like water
in the chest of a drowned man. There's nothing

to do but give him something soft to hold
—say, a bale of wool—to convince him

to inhale anyway. This man is no different.

He lies prone in the field.
A shepherd sits next to him,

taking in the scene, waiting.

Eye-level with the flora, now a yard high,
a pink plane hovering above green as far

as the land goes, the flat yolk of daisies suspended
in misty albumin; the sheep so white, so dense,

you might confuse them—if you only ever gazed
forward, and never up—for the clouds themselves;

the clouds like eggshells, holding color only
in their creases, the places where fingers pried

them apart; thin green streams where some soul
tried to suture them back together with strings of grass;

here, the shepherd arrived the same way. Flat on his back,
unblinking. With nothing more than the seeds

in the treads of his shoes, he sprung rich pasture
from the badlands in which he awakened.

Sewed echinacea, and orchids, and gerbera—florae
that produce the most oxygen. A garden that almost respires

enough to keep a man alive on its own.

\\\

As the new man begins his undeath, the shepherd turns
him on his side, leaning against him, the razed fields

of their backs for a time married. With his cloak,
he wipes the tears that dry down like chalky gypsum

on the new man's cheeks. Finished coughing out the past,
the new man stills. The meadow inhales deeply, huffs to attention.

Good morning, the shepherd offers, as if there,
it is always morning, always day brimming

on the edge of some true tomorrow.

I'm Eric.

The shepherd pulls on his cigarette—pursing his lips
to reveal an interior pink, as he blows a slight white

stream into the crisp bluster—extends it to his guest.
The new man reaches for the stub

and their hands meet without touching, like wind
through stiff reeds, their slight bend the only proof

of any contact at all. The new man whispers
his name with a lungfull of smoke.

> *George*, he hums. *I'm George.*

> A pause. *Is this heaven?*

> Eric exhales. *It ain't earth. For now, for me, that's enough.*

George nods. They breathe in tandem
with the field; inhale, exhale, and again—

Love Poem in the Black Field

the burning streets of America, 19–, 20–

68

And what, my love, but the pasture?
      But the blades refusing to brown
Beneath this wintered march?
      What else, in this world, can still call
Itself *living?* Teach me how
      To consider the lilies; all they are
Because of, all they are despite.
      How you delight in their opening:
A glacial flick, like a snake's split
      Tongue. I want, like you, not to seek
The beast in every bud. To see
      A field of men as yet a field.
Black though it may be. But here
      I am, the wilt of the meadow.
My young body already yellow with bitter
      Spots. Show me what is untouched
By the godless blue. What here was sewn
      With any sense of grace.
As we scrape raw our throats, crack our fists
      Against this steeling air; the teargas,
Like craneflies ambling around dim
      Porchlights, drifts lower, my flesh
Begs, *what else but this suffering*
      Has made me worthy of your hands?
As you turn my tears to milk, calm
      My lungs with purple aster; as you wait
'Til the remedy turns sweet enough
      To kiss from my lips, your breath
Answers: *we are weed and flower, both.*
      Reminds me how we were soft once,

In His grasp, before the plough
        Split our napes. Before these iron barbs
Took root. And I am surer, now,
        Of my ugliness, and surer that I love you
Because you don't try to make me
        Unknow this truth. The sirens,
The boots, they stampede on. But we alive
        Because of—we alive despite.

Sweet Field Anemola

anemoia (n.)—nostalgia for a time you've never known

70

There was, at one time, an empty field. I'm sure of it.
Or, was it a forest so jade that a vine snake's darting
left only glare, like light breaking over rolling grain. . .

No, I know there was a field because I miss it—
its brush languid as a forest slinking into jaded slumber,
dragging floor dwellers at its outskirts like a tulle train,

the land trodden by what once bent its grasses with breath.
God, what we could do without yesterday, its forested jaundice,
its sepia fog. With the prologue we ourselves sowed, a terrain

thick with memory of unbodied lush. Florid.
A forest of stalks. Weeping, it shone like jade
in the easy sun. Yes, there was warmth. Sugarcane.

A sweetness. Or even just its thick simulacra. It whispered
like sound in an adjacent forest, an aria unflattened
by my failure to prove it real. . . Believe me. I'm sane,

I swear. I remember the pasture, the soft sickle
of a new leaf. Each shoot its own forest with only jaybirds
and lace bugs coming between stems and their rain.

Listen, I know this field. It never held a soul. No tree
-bark backs. No forest of bowed limbs. No blue jaws.
No ambered-over sores. Only green thoughts. Only the mundane.

NOTES

"Epithalamion in the Wake" is set within the Middle Passage of the transatlantic slave trade, during which millions of Africans were brought, on ships, to the Americas for enslavement.

"things tiny enough to fit through Elmina's door of no return" references Elmina Castle, a stronghold of the Portuguese on Ghana's Cape Coast.

"Strange Fruit Market" explores the history of pineapple—in colonial America, pineapple was served as a symbol of hospitality. In Ghana, enslaved captives used wild pineapples to mark their path to Assin Manso, the last stop before the Middle Passage.

"Said the Tobacco to the Hand" explores Virginia's largest cash crop; by 1700, enslaved Africans outnumbered white indentured servants, becoming the primary source of labor for the cultivation of tobacco, so proliferous that twenty-two million pounds were shipped from Virginia to England that year.

"Dear Moses Grandy. . . Love, the Great Dismal Swamp" is written to Captain Moses Grandy, an enslaved Black man largely responsible for carving the untamed swampland into a canal that became a crucial venue for travel and commerce. The first epigraph is taken from the *Smithsonian Magazine* article "Deep in the Swamps, Archaeologists Are Finding How Fugitive Slaves Kept Their Freedom" by Richard Grant. The second epigraph is a quote from Grandy himself, taken from his *Narrative of the Life of Moses Grandy; Late a Slave in the United States of America* (London: C. Gilpin, 1843).

"Boll Weevil's Theodicy" centers on the boll weevil, an invasive insect that migrated north from Mexico and Central America in the late nineteenth century, effectively destroying the cotton trade that had powered the Southern economy via slavery and, later, sharecropping, for centuries. The epigraph is taken from "The Strange Affair of the Boll Weevil: The Pest as Liberator" by Dr. Arvarh E. Strickland, published in *Agricultural History*, vol. 68.

"Antipastoral: This Green and Pleasant Land" draws its title and inspiration from both Vievee Francis's "Anti-Pastoral" and British photographer and artist Ingrid Pollard's *A Green and Pleasant Land*.

The epigraph in "How to Run Away" was taken from *Shadows in Silver: VIRGINIA 1850–1900, People, Plantations, Towns and Cities, A Pictorial Record of Virginia*, and captions a photograph of young farm boys searching the fields for rodents and rabbits to catch and eat.

"Love Poem in the Black Field (III)" takes place at Parchman Farm, the site of one of the earliest chain gangs, in which Black prisoners were shackled together and forced to perform manual labor.

"Rorschach After the Storm" is inspired by visual artist Julie Mehretu's *Epigraph, Damascus* (2016, photogravure, etching, and aquatint, 97⅝ × 226 in., Whitney Museum of American Art, New York).

"Still Life with Bouquet, Golden Spade (out of frame)" is a riff on Terrance Hayes' "Golden Shovel," which takes the last word of each of its lines from a Gwendolyn Brooks' poem "We Real Cool." This Golden Spade also uses the words from Brooks' poem progressively later in each line to create a diagonal throughline. It is also inspired by painter Jennifer Packer's *Say Her Name* (2017, oil on canvas, 48 × 40, Whitney Museum of American Art, New York).

"Hotbeds in Norfolk, Virginia" references Frank O'Hara's love poem, "Mary Desti's Ass."

"Game Theory" was written in the resounding echo of Camille Dungy's "Trophic Cascade."

"Still Life with Tulip as Grenade" is about a March 2021 incident, covered in *The Herald Sun* by Virginia Bridges ("North Carolina sends 6-year-olds to court. Why some say it's time for change."), in which a six-year-old Black boy in Durham, North Carolina was arrested and charged with "damage to real property" for picking a tulip out of a woman's yard as he waited for the school bus one morning.

"No. 2 (No. 7 and No. 2): oil on canvas: Mark Rothko: 1951" takes inspiration from one of Rothko's famed color field paintings. It was written in remembrance of Eric Garner and George Floyd.

"Sweet Field Anemoia" takes its title from a term found in John Koenig's *The Dictionary of Obscure Sorrows*.

ACKNOWLEDGMENTS

Love and gratitude to the following journals and anthologies (in order of appearance) in which some versions of the poems in this collection were published: *Copper Nickel, Academy of American Poets University & College Prizes, POETRY, Shenandoah, Aunt Chloe: A Journal of Artful Candor, World Literature Today, Obsidian, EcoTheo Review, Academy of American Poets Poem-a-Day, Transition Magazine, Magma, Black Warrior Review, Indiana Review, The Yale Review, Porter House Review, Beyond the Frame (Diode Editions Anthology), Tinderbox, Southern Humanities Review,* and *Colorado Review.*

Love to my family, my pillars; to Donovan and Chenell, you inspire me always; to Kéla, my *person*; to Obsidian Group E, who believe, and so make me believe; to Sharan Strange, my truest teacher, in every sense of the word; to Dr. Gloria Wade Gayles, who taught me to tend the muses; to Recinda McGovern, who sowed a belief in me from which I will always reap courage; to Elyce Strong Mann, who gave me a path to follow and showed me how to make my own; to Dr. Michelle Hite, who gives me permission to be unruly, on and off the page; to Remica Bingham-Risher, for whom my love and admiration run so much deeper than the blood we share.

Love to all those without whom this collection would not exist, especially Redell Olsen, Vievee Francis, Patricia Smith, Amber Flora Thomas, Mahtem Shifferraw, my Marshall Scholarship friends, the Rhino crash, my cohorts at Tin House, Palm Beach Poetry Festival, Mendocino Coast Writers' Conference, Middlebury Bread Loaf Environmental Workshop, The Seventh Wave, and the Obsidian Foundation in the United Kingdom.

Love to Beth Snead, Lea Johnson, and the wonderful editorial and design teams at University of Georgia Press; to Cave Canem—all its history upon which this book stands; to Willie Perdomo for seeing a special beauty in these poems before they became a book.

Love to my parents, who have always been there to bend away the branches in my path, who taught me what it means to make a way.

Love to my granddad, who taught me, if nothing else, to love this land, this earth that we shared for only two short days.

Love to all those who loved me into being, and who will love me into whatever lies beyond.

Printed in the United States
by Baker & Taylor Publisher Services